Craven – Pamlico – Carteret
Regional Library

Hot or Not?

Nicola Baxter

CHILDRENS PRESS ®

CHICAGO

Would you like to live somewhere very, very hot?

Would you like to live somewhere very, very cold?

What is hot?

Running quickly can make you feel hot.
But you are not as hot as a very hot drink.

And your hot drink is not as hot as the fire in your fireplace.

nd nothing on Earth is as hot as the sun.
he sun is so hot that we can feel its heat
lthough it is millions of miles away.

There is some heat in everything on Earth, even in things that seem cold.

Things that have a lot of heat feel hotter than things that have less heat.

Try this...
Put some cold water in a plastic mug.
Put cold water and ice cubes in another plastic mug

Dip your finger in the mug of water. How does it feel?
Dip the same finger in the ice water.
How does that feel?
Then dip your finger in the first mug again.
Does it feel warmer? Does it feel colder?

We cannot see heat, but sometimes we can see how heat changes things.

What is making the strawberry ice cream change?

The air has more heat than the ice cream and warms it up.

What might happen to a snowman on a warm, sunny day?
Do you think the snowman would melt quickly or slowly?

Heat always likes to escape!
It tries to move out of something hot
and into something cooler.

Try this...
Fill a bowl with warm water.
After half an hour, feel how hot the water is.
Has some of the heat in the water escaped?
Where do you think it has gone?

To keep something warm,
we have to stop its heat from escaping.
Which bowl of food do you think will
stay hot longer?

People need to keep warm.
If it is very cold outside, the heat
inside our bodies tries to escape.

We wear clothes to keep the heat inside.

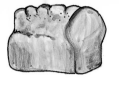

Something gets colder when heat escapes from it.
It gets hotter when more heat moves into it.
Heat can change sticky, white dough into tasty brown bread!

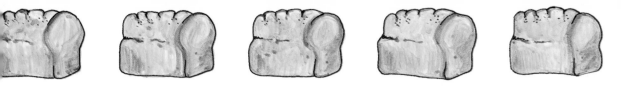

We can use heat to help us.
But always be very careful with hot thing
Do not touch hot things without the help
of a grownup.

What are the children using to help them
get ready for a party?

Very, very high heat can melt metal.

Heat can be measured with a thermometer.

It shows how hot it is outside, or even how hot it is inside you!

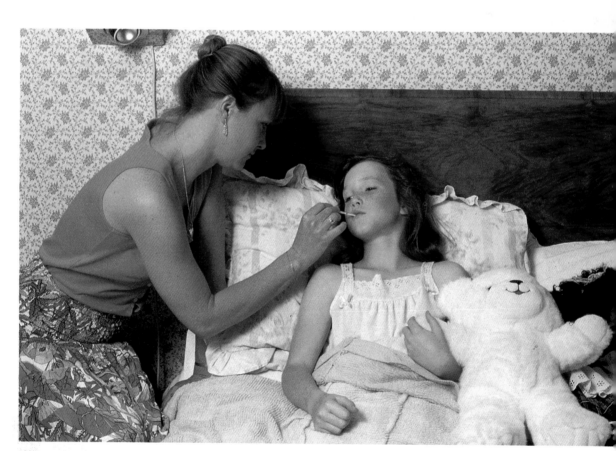

Try this...

Make a chart to show how hot or cold it is today.
Is it hotter or colder than yesterday?
Move the arrow up or down.
A grownup can help you look at a thermometer
to see if you are right.

Look at the picture.
Which things might be hot and which might not?
Which should you be careful not to touc

Now look around you.
What is the hottest thing you can see?

bread, 16

clothes, 14
cold, 3, 8, 9, 14, 21

dough, 16
drink, 4, 6

Earth, 7, 8

fire, 6
fireplace, 6
food, 13

heat, 7, 8, 9, 10, 12, 13, 14, 16, 18, 19, 20

hot, 2, 4, 6, 7, 12, 13, 18, 20, 21, 22
ice, 9
ice cream, 10

metal, 19

snowman, 11
sun, 7

thermometer, 20, 21

warm, 11, 12, 13, 14
water, 9, 12

1996 Childrens Press Edition
© 1995 Watts Books

All rights reserved
Published simultaneously in Canada

1 2 3 4 5 6 7 8 9 10 00 99 98 97 96

Editor: Sarah Ridley
Designer: Nina Kingsbury
Photographer: Peter Millard
Illustrator: Michael Evans

Library of Congress Cataloging-in-Publication Data

Baxter, Nicola.
  Hot or not / by Nicola Baxter; illustrated by Michael Evans.
    p. cm. – (Toppers)
    ISBN 0-516-09267-7
1. Heat–Juvenile literature. 2. Heat–Experiments –Juvenile literature. 3. Cold–Juvenile literature. 4. Cold–Experiments. 5. Experiments.] I. Evans, Michael. 1966- ill. II. Title. III. Series: Baxter, Nicola. Toppers.
  QC256.B39 1995
  536–dc20   94-44719 CIP AC

The publishers would like to thank Carol Olivier, Lateefah Elcock,

Osbert Clements and Leanne Bates of Kenmont Primary Sch for their help with this book.

Additional photographs: B & C Alexander, 3; Bubbles Photo Library, 20; James Davis Trave Photography, 8; Robert Hardir Picture Library, 7, 19; Hutchisc Library, 2.

Printed in Malaysia

2-2000